Pasta Cookbook: Famil
Everyday Pasta R(
Inspired by The Mediter

by Alissa Noel Grey

Text copyright(c)2016 Alissa Noel Grey

All rights reserved. No part of this publication may be reproduced, distributed, or transmitted in any form or by any means, including photocopying, recording, or other electronic or mechanical methods, without the prior written permission of the publisher, except in the case of brief quotations embodied in critical reviews and certain other noncommercial uses permitted by copyright law.

Although every precaution has been taken to verify the accuracy of the information contained herein, the author and publisher assume no responsibility for any errors or omissions. No liability is assumed for damages that may result from the use of information contained within.

Table Of Contents

Everyday Pasta Meals, Salads and Sauces Inspired by the Mediterranean Diet	4
Mediterranean Chicken and Pasta Salad	5
Summer Pasta Salad	6
Caprese-style Pasta Salad	7
Superfood Macaroni Salad	8
Pea and Orzo Salad	9
Tuna Pasta Salad	10
Tuna and Mushroom Pasta Salad	11
Mediterranean Spaghetti Bolognaise	12
Roasted Pepper Pasta	14
Simple Eggplant Pasta	15
Pasta Arrabiata	16
Orzo with Brussels Sprouts and Sausage	17
Farfalle with Watercress, Cherry Tomatoes, and Feta	18
Avocado and Arugula Pasta	19
Creamy Avocado and Chicken Spaghetti	20
Avocado, Roasted Mushroom and Ham Spaghetti	21
Avocado, Roasted Mushroom and Tuna Spaghetti	22
One-Pot Vegan Pasta	23
Bean and Pasta Soup	24
Tomato, Arugula and Feta Spaghetti	25
Easy Summer Spaghetti	26
Lentil and Olive Spaghetti	27
Pasta with Kale, Garlic and Cheese	28
One-Pot Pizza Pasta	29
Easy Summer Spaghetti	30
One-Pot Tomato Basil Pasta	31
Delicious Zucchini Pasta	32
Pasta alla Genovese	33
Pasta with Asparagus	34
Easy One-Pot Spaghetti	35
Hearty Lentil Spaghetti	36
One-Pot Pasta Peperonata	37
Mini Shell Bacon and Pea Pasta	38

Pasta with Chicken and Broccoli Pesto	39
One-Pot Pasta a La Puttanesca	40
Ground Beef Pasta with Garlic-Yogurt Sauce	41
Easy Homemade Lasagna	42
Beef and Spinach Lasagna	44
Baked Ground Beef Pasta	46
Baked Pasta with Broccoli, Olives and Pancetta	48
Baked Penne with with Spinach, Feta and Fontina	50
Easy Three-Cheese Pasta with Chicken and Mushrooms	51
Greek-style Baked Pasta	53
Ricotta and Spinach Cannelloni	55
FREE BONUS RECIPES: 20 Superfood Paleo and Vegan Smoothies for Vibrant Health and Easy Weight Loss	57
Kale and Kiwi Smoothie	58
Delicious Broccoli Smoothie	59
Papaya Smoothie	60
Beet and Papaya Smoothie	61
Lean Green Smoothie	62
Easy Antioxidant Smoothie	63
Healthy Purple Smoothie	64
Mom's Favorite Kale Smoothie	65
Creamy Green Smoothie	66
Strawberry and Arugula Smoothie	67
Emma's Amazing Smoothie	68
Good-To-Go Morning Smoothie	69
Endless Energy Smoothie	70
High-fibre Fruit Smoothie	71
Nutritious Green Smoothie	72
Apricot, Strawberry and Banana Smoothie	73
Spinach and Green Apple Smoothie	74
Superfood Blueberry Smoothie	75
Zucchini and Blueberry Smoothie	76
Tropical Spinach Smoothie	77

Everyday Pasta Meals, Salads and Sauces Inspired by the Mediterranean Diet

Pasta meals are central to the Mediterranean Diet because they are tasty, inexpensive and easy to prepare, and also because they are the perfect way to highlight many of the other healthy foods in this diet. In Mediterranean countries pasta is usually eaten with delicious superfood partners, such as fiber-rich vegetables and legumes, heart-healthy fish, olives and olive oil, antioxidant-rich tomato sauce and protein-packed lean meats, poultry, and cheeses.

Pasta is inexpensive, fast to cook, and you can serve it in a million different ways. Pasta can absolutely be part of a healthy diet too. It is fat-free, low sodium and can fill you up so you don't feel hungry. Pasta has a low Glycemic Index (GI) and does not cause sugar in the blood to rise quickly.

Pasta made from whole-grain flour is an even better option as it contains more fiber and nutrients than white-flour varieties and is increasingly easy to find on grocery shelves and in restaurants.

To create healthy pasta meals you just have to use it as a base for dishes rich in vegetables, lean proteins and healthy fats. It is best to replace heavy sauces with low-calorie vegetable-based versions, such as fresh tomato sauce or a light basil or broccoli pesto. You can also use simple dressings prepared at home with fresh herbs, garlic, lemon juice and drizzle of olive oil. A good trick to promote weight loss is to replace ½ or ¼ of your pasta meal with beans, chickpeas or lentils.

Pasta is a filling, cheap, and easy meal that also tastes great! The recipes included in this book are very easy to follow, fun to prepare, and will help you look like a professional pasta chef.

As with everything, enjoy pasta in moderation - be mindful of portion sizes and experiment with all the glorious varieties!

Mediterranean Chicken and Pasta Salad

Serves: 5-6

Prep time: 5 min

Ingredients:

3 cups small pasta, cooked

3 chicken breast halves, cooked and shredded

1 cup cherry tomatoes, halved

1 yellow bell pepper, sliced

1 small red onion, sliced

1/2 cup black olives, pitted

2 tbsp capers

1/3 cup pine nuts, toasted

7-8 fresh basil leaves, finely chopped

for the dressing:

1/4 cup lemon juice

1/4 cup extra virgin olive oil

2 garlic cloves, crushed

salt, to taste

Directions:

Place pasta, chicken, tomatoes, bell pepper, red onion, basil, olives, capers and pine nuts in a large bowl.

Prepare the dressing by whisking lemon juice, olive oil, garlic and salt. Pour the dressing over the salad, toss to combine, and serve.

Summer Pasta Salad

Serves 5-6

Prep time 25 min

Ingredients:

2 cups small pasta

2 hard boiled eggs, peeled and diced

1 cup ham, diced

1 red bell pepper, thinly sliced

1-2 spring onions, finely cut

1 tbsp fresh dill, chopped

1/2 cup mayonnaise

2 tbsp lemon juice

freshly ground black pepper, to taste

Directions:

Cook pasta as directed on package. When cooked through but al dente, remove from heat, drain and rinse.

Put the onions into a salad bowl and toss with the lemon juice. Add in the ham, pasta and all other ingredients.

Season with salt and pepper to taste and serve.

Caprese-style Pasta Salad

Serves 5-6

Prep time 25 min

Ingredients:

3 cups small pasta

1 cup baby mozzarella

2 cups cherry tomatoes, halved

1-2 spring onions, finely cut

4 tbsp basil pesto

3 tbsp white balsamic vinegar

2-3 tbsp extra virgin olive oil

Directions:

Cook pasta as directed on package. When cooked through but al dente, remove from heat, drain and rinse.

Combine pesto, olive oil and vinegar in a small cup.

Place tomatoes, mozzarella, spring onions and cooled pasta in a salad bowl. Season with salt and pepper. Add pesto mixture. Toss to combine and serve.

Superfood Macaroni Salad

Serves 5-6

Prep time 25 min

Ingredients:

2 cups macaroni

2 oz smoked salmon

2 cups baby spinach

2 boiled eggs, chopped

1 cup mayonnaise

4-5 green onions, finely cut

1 garlic clove, crushed

3 tbsp lemon juice

salt and black pepper, to taste

Directions:

Cook macaroni as directed on package. When cooked through but al dente, remove from heat, drain and rinse.

Combine the mayonnaise, garlic and lemon juice in a bowl. Add the eggs, salmon, onions and spinach and toss to coat with the dressing. Season with salt and freshly ground pepper to taste.

Pea and Orzo Salad

Serves 5-6

Prep time 25 min

Ingredients:

1 cup orzo

2 cups frozen peas

1 cup finely cut parsley leaves

1-2 spring onions, finely cut

4 tbsp basil pesto

3 tbsp white balsamic vinegar

2-3 tbsp extra virgin olive oil

Directions:

Cook orzo in a large saucepan of boiling, salted water, following packet directions until tender. Add peas in the last 3 minutes of cooking. Drain well and return to pot.

Combine pesto, olive oil and vinegar in a small cup and pour over the orzo mixture. Stir in parsley and serve.

Tuna Pasta Salad

Serves 5-6

Prep time 25 min

Ingredients:

2 cups small pasta

2 hard boiled eggs, peeled and diced

1 can tuna in oil, drained, flaked

1 cup cherry tomatoes, halved

1 cucumber, peeled and diced

1-2 spring onions, finely cut

2 tbsp fresh parsley, chopped

3 tbsp extra virgin olive oil

2 tbsp lemon juice

1 tsp lemon zest

salt and freshly ground black pepper, to taste

Directions:

Cook pasta as directed on package. When cooked through but al dente, remove from heat, drain and rinse.

Combine lemon zest, lemon juice, oil and salt and pepper in a cup.

Add tuna, eggs, tomatoes, cucumber and parsley to pasta. Pour over dressing and toss until well combined.

Tuna and Mushroom Pasta Salad

Serves 5-6

Prep time 25 min

Ingredients:

2 cups small pasta

10 white button mushrooms, sliced

1 can tuna in oil, drained, flaked

1 red pepper, chopped

1 large apple, peeled and diced

4-5 spring onions, finely cut

1/3 cup mayonnaise

2 tbsp lemon juice

salt and freshly ground black pepper, to taste

Directions:

Cook pasta as directed on package. When cooked through but al dente, remove from heat, drain and rinse.

Combine mayonnaise, lemon juice, oil and salt and pepper in a cup.

Add tuna, apple, pepper and mushrooms to pasta. Pour over dressing and toss until well combined.

Mediterranean Spaghetti Bolognaise

Serves 6

Prep time: 20 min

Ingredients:

17 oz spaghetti

1 lb ground beef

1 onion, chopped

2 garlic cloves, finely chopped

2 tbsp tomato paste

1 can tomatoes, diced, undrained

1/3 cup dried tomatoes, chopped

1/2 cup black olives, pitted, halved

1/4 cup chopped fresh basil leaves

1 tsp dried oregano

Parmesan cheese, to serve

salt and pepper, to taste

Directions:

Heat oil in a large saucepan over medium-high heat. Add ground beef, onion and garlic. Cook, stirring, for 7-8 minutes, or until the meat has browned.

Add tomato paste, tomatoes, dried tomatoes, olives, basil, and oregano and simmer for 10 minutes, or until thickened. Season with salt and pepper.

Prepare spaghetti as described on package directions.

Wash, drain and divide them between bowls. Top with sauce and sprinkle with Parmesan cheese and fresh basil leaves.

Roasted Pepper Pasta

Serves: 4-5

Prep time: 30 min

Ingredients:

12 oz small pasta

4-5 red peppers, halved and de-seeded

1 cup cherry tomatoes

3-4 garlic cloves, sliced

3 tbsp olive oil

1/2 tsp sugar

5-6 tbsp pesto

Parmesan cheese, to serve

Directions:

Line a baking tray with baking paper and place the peppers, tomatoes and garlic on it. Sprinkle with olive oil and sugar and season with salt and black pepper to taste.

Roast in a preheated to 375 F oven for 15 minutes, or until the vegetables are slightly charred around the edges.

Prepare the pasta according to package directions. Toss it with the roasted vegetables and serve with pesto and Parmesan cheese.

Simple Eggplant Pasta

Serves 6

Prep time: 20 min

Ingredients:

12 oz rigatoni

1 lb ground beef

1/2 onion, finely cut

2 garlic cloves, finely chopped

1 small eggplant, peeled and diced

1 can tomatoes, diced, undrained

1/4 cup chopped fresh basil leaves

a pinch of chilli flakes

3 tbsp extra virgin olive oil

Parmesan cheese, to serve

salt and pepper, to taste

Directions:

Heat oil in a large saucepan over medium-high heat. Add ground beef, onion, garlic and eggplant. Cook, stirring, for 7-8 minutes, or until the meat has browned.

Add in tomatoes, basil, and chilli and simmer for 10-15 minutes, or until thickened. Season with salt and pepper.

Prepare pasta as described on package directions. Wash, drain and divide it between bowls. Top with sauce and sprinkle with Parmesan cheese and fresh basil leaves.

Pasta Arrabiata

Serves 6

Prep time: 20 min

Ingredients:

12 oz rigatoni

3-4 slices salami, chopped

1/2 onion, finely cut

2 garlic cloves, finely chopped

1 can tomatoes, diced, undrained

1/4 cup chopped fresh basil leaves

1/4 tsp of chilli flakes

1/2 tsp dried oregano

3 tbsp extra virgin olive oil

Parmesan cheese, to serve

salt and pepper, to taste

Directions:

Heat oil in a large saucepan over medium-high heat. Add onion and salami. Cook for 3- 4 minutes or until onion has softened. Add in garlic and chilli. Cook until fragrant.

Add tomatoes and oregano and bring to a simmer. Simmer for 2-3 minutes or until slightly thickened. Season with salt and pepper.

Prepare pasta as described on package directions. Add it to tomato mixture and toss to combine. Serve with Parmesan.

Orzo with Brussels Sprouts and Sausage

Serves 6

Prep time: 20 min

Ingredients:

1 cup orzo

2 cups shredded or chopped Brussels sprouts

1/2 onion, finely cut

1/2 lb loose pork sausage

3 tbsp sour cream

2 tbsp extra virgin olive oil

Parmesan cheese, to serve

2-3 fresh basil leaves

salt and pepper, to taste

Directions:

Heat oil in a large saucepan over medium-high heat. Add onion, sausage and Brussels sprouts. Cook, stirring, for 7-8 minutes, or until the sausage has browned. Stir in sour cream.

Prepare orzo as described on package directions. Wash, drain and add it to Brussels spout mixture. Top with Parmesan cheese and fresh basil leaves.

Farfalle with Watercress, Cherry Tomatoes, and Feta

Serves 6

Prep time: 20 min

Ingredients:

8 oz farfalle pasta

1 cup crumbled feta cheese

2 cups cherry tomatoes, halved

3 cups watercress leaves

1 cup black olives, pitted

salt and pepper, to taste

Directions:

Prepare pasta as described on package directions. Place the tomatoes in a colander and drain the pasta over them for a super-quick blanch.

Place the cheese in a large bowl; top with the watercress, tomatoes, pasta and olives. Season with salt and pepper to taste, toss to combine, and serve.

Avocado and Arugula Pasta

Serves: 4

Prep time: 5 min

Ingredients:

3 cups cooked bow tie pasta

½ cup cooked corn kernels

1 large avocado, peeled and diced

1 cup baby arugula leaves

2 tbsp basil pesto

3 tbsp extra virgin olive oil

3 tbsp lemon juice

½ cup grated Parmesan cheese

Directions:

Whisk olive oil, lemon juice, basil pesto and half the Parmesan cheese in a small bowl. Season with salt and pepper to taste.

Combine pasta, avocado, corn and baby arugula. Add oil mixture and toss to combine. Serve with remaining Parmesan cheese.

Creamy Avocado and Chicken Spaghetti

Serves: 5-6

Prep time: 20 min

Ingredients:

12 oz spaghetti

1 cup cooked chicken, shredded

2 avocados, peeled and diced

1 cup cherry tomatoes, halved

1 garlic clove, chopped

2 tbsp basil pesto

5 tbsp olive oil

4 tbsp lemon juice

1/4 cup grated Parmesan cheese

Directions:

In a large pot of boiling salted water, cook spaghetti according to package instructions. Drain and set aside in a large bowl.

In a blender, combine lemon juice, garlic, basil pesto and avocados and blend until smooth.

Combine spaghetti, chicken, cherry tomatoes and avocado sauce. Sprinkle with Parmesan cheese and serve immediately.

Avocado, Roasted Mushroom and Ham Spaghetti

Serves: 5-6

Prep time: 20 min

Ingredients:

12 oz spaghetti

1 cup ham, cut in cubes

2 avocados, peeled and diced

10-15 white mushrooms, halved

2 tbsp green olive paste

2 garlic cloves, chopped

olive oil spay

salt and black pepper, to taste

1/4 cup grated Parmesan cheese

Directions:

Line a baking tray with baking paper and place mushrooms on it. Spray with olive oil and season with salt and black pepper to taste. Roast in a preheated to 375 F oven for 15 minutes, or until golden and tender.

In a large pot of boiling salted water, cook spaghetti according to package instructions. Drain and set aside in a large bowl.

In a blender, combine lemon juice, garlic, olive paste and avocados and blend until smooth.

Combine pasta, diced ham, mushrooms and avocado sauce. Sprinkle with Parmesan cheese and serve immediately.

Avocado, Roasted Mushroom and Tuna Spaghetti

Serves: 5-6

Prep time: 20 min

Ingredients:

12 oz whole wheat spaghetti

1 can tuna, drained and broken into small chunks

2 avocados, peeled and diced

10-15 white mushrooms, halved

5-6 green onions, finely cut

2 garlic cloves, chopped

4 tbsp lemon or lime juice

olive oil spay

salt and black pepper, to taste

Directions:

Line a baking tray with baking paper and place the mushrooms on it. Spray with olive oil and season with salt and black pepper to taste. Roast in a preheated to 375 F oven for 15 minutes, or until golden and tender.

In a large pot of boiling salted water, cook spaghetti according to package instructions. Drain and set aside in a large bowl.

In a blender, combine the lemon juice, garlic, and avocados and blend until smooth.

Combine spaghetti, tuna, roasted mushrooms and avocado sauce. Sprinkle with green onions and serve immediately.

One-Pot Vegan Pasta

Serves: 4-5

Ingredients:

12 oz dry pasta

1/2 onion, chopped

1/2 small eggplant, peeled and cubed

1 small zucchini, peeled and cubed

1 garlic clove, crushed

1.5 cups vegan marinara sauce

2 cups water

3 tbsp olive oil

1/3 cup fresh parsley, finely cut

1 tsp salt

1 tsp fresh black pepper

Directions:

Heat a large saucepan over medium-high heat. Add in olive oil and gently saute the onion. Stir in eggplant, garlic, the zucchini, pasta, water, marinara sauce, and season with salt and black pepper.

Bring to a boil, then cover and reduce heat to a simmer until the pasta is cooked to al dente. Sprinkle with parsley, adjust seasonings, and serve.

Bean and Pasta Soup

Serves: 4-5

Prep time: 10-15 min

Ingredients:

1 onion, chopped

2 large carrots, chopped

2 garlic cloves, minced

1 cup cooked orzo

1 15 oz can white beans, rinsed and drained

1 15 oz can tomatoes, diced and undrained

1 cup baby spinach leaves

3 cups chicken broth

1 tbsp paprika

1 tbsp dried mint

3 tbsp extra virgin olive oil

salt and black pepper, to taste

Directions:

Heat the olive oil over medium heat and gently sauté the onion, garlic and carrots. Add in tomatoes, broth, salt and pepper, and bring to a boil.

Reduce heat and cook for 5-10 minutes, or until the carrots are tender. Stir in orzo, beans and spinach, and simmer until spinach is wilted.

Tomato, Arugula and Feta Spaghetti

Serves: 5-6

Prep time: 20 min

Ingredients:

12 oz spaghetti

2 cups grape tomatoes, halved

1 cup fresh basil leaves, roughly torn

1 cup baby arugula leaves

1 cup feta, crumbled

2 garlic cloves, chopped

5 tbsp extra virgin olive oil

salt and black pepper, to taste

Directions:

In a large saucepan of boiling salted water, cook spaghetti according to package instructions. Drain and set aside in a large bowl.

Return saucepan to medium heat. Add olive oil, garlic and tomatoes. Season with black pepper and cook, tossing, for 1-2 minutes or until tomatoes are hot. Add spaghetti, basil and feta. Toss gently for 1 minute or until heated through. Top with arugula and serve.

Easy Summer Spaghetti

Serves: 4-5

Ingredients:

12 oz spaghetti

1/2 onion, chopped

1 green pepper, sliced

1 cup cooked chicken, shredded or diced

1/3 can chickpeas, drained

1/2 cup black olives, pitted and halved

2 garlic cloves, crushed

1.5 cups marinara sauce

2 cups water

3 tbsp extra virgin olive oil

1/3 cup fresh parsley, finely cut

1/4 cup grated Parmesan cheese

Directions:

Heat a large saucepan over medium-high heat. Add in olive oil and gently saute the onion. Stir in the pepper, chicken, olives and chickpeas and cook, stirring, for 2-3 minutes.

Add in water and marinara sauce and season with salt and black pepper.

Bring to a boil, then add spaghetti and stir. Reduce heat and simmer until the spaghetti is cooked to al dente. Sprinkle with parsley, adjust seasonings, and serve with Paremsan cheese.

Lentil and Olive Spaghetti

Serves: 4-5

Ingredients:

12 oz spaghetti

1/2 onion, chopped

1 can brown lentils, rinsed, drained

1 cup black olives, pitted and halved

2 garlic cloves, crushed

2 cups marinara sauce

2 cups water

3 tbsp olive oil

1/3 cup fresh mint, finely cut

1 tsp salt

Directions:

Heat a large saucepan over medium-high heat. Add in olive oil and gently saute the onion. Stir in garlic, lentils, olives, water, marinara sauce, and season with salt and black pepper.

Bring to a boil, then add spaghetti and stir. Reduce heat and simmer until the spaghetti is cooked to al dente.

Sprinkle with mint, adjust seasonings, and serve.

Pasta with Kale, Garlic and Cheese

Serves: 4-5

Ingredients:

12 oz spaghetti

2 cups curly kale, chopped

5-6 sun-dried tomatoes

2 garlic cloves, crushed

3 tbsp olive oil

1 cup crumbled feta cheese, to serve

Directions:

Prepare the pasta according to package directions.

Put the kale in a colander and pour over 3 cups of boiling water of water. Leave to drain.

In a deep saucepan, gently heat olive oil and add the garlic and kale. Cook for about 3-4 minutes until tender. Drain the pasta and add to the pan with the sun-dried tomatoes.

Toss everything well, sprinkle with feta cheese and serve.

One-Pot Pizza Pasta

Serves: 4

Prep time 35 min

Ingredients:

1 pound Italian sausage, casings removed if necessary

8 oz penne pasta

1/3 cup onion, finely chopped

1/2 cup ham, diced

1/2 cup red bell pepper, chopped

1 (24 oz) jar spaghetti sauce

1 can diced tomatoes

3-4 green or black olives

1 cup grated cheese

salt and black pepper, to taste

a handful of baby rocket leaves, to serve

Directions:

Heat a large skillet on medium heat and sauté the onion, ham, sausage and red pepper for 1-2 minutes.

Add in the spaghetti sauce, diced tomatoes, water, and olives. Stir to combine. Add in the pasta and carefully stir to combine again.

Cover and simmer for 10-15 minutes or until the pasta is tender.

Preheat the broiler. Top pasta with shredded cheese and pepperoni. Place under broiler for 3-5 minutes or until cheese is melted.

Easy Summer Spaghetti

Serves: 5-6

Prep time: 20 min

Ingredients:

12 oz whole-wheat spaghetti

2-3 spring onions, finely cut

1 small zucchini, peeled and diced

1 small eggplant, peeled and diced

1/2 cup canned chickpeas, drained

1/2 cup black olives, pitted and halved

2 garlic cloves, crushed

1.5 cups tomato sauce

2 cups water

3 tbsp extra virgin olive oil

1 tsp dried basil

1/3 cup fresh parsley, finely cut

1 tsp salt

Directions:

Heat a deep saucepan over medium-high heat. Add in olive oil and gently saute the spring onion and garlic for 1 minute, stirring.

Add in the olives, chickpeas, eggplant, zucchini, water, tomato sauce, basil, and season with salt and black pepper.

Bring to a boil, add spaghetti and stir. Reduce heat and cook until the spaghetti is cooked to al dente.

Sprinkle with parsley, adjust seasonings, and serve.

One-Pot Tomato Basil Pasta

Serves: 4

Prep time 20 min

Ingredients:

12 oz small pasta

12 oz cherry tomatoes, halved

1 cup onion, finely cut

2 cloves garlic, chopped

1 tbsp tomato paste

1/2 tsp paprika

1 cup fresh basil leaves, finely cut

2 tbsp extra virgin olive oil

salt and freshly ground pepper, to taste

4 1/2 cups water

extra virgin olive oil, to serve

freshly grated Parmesan cheese, to serve

Directions:

Combine pasta, tomatoes, onion, garlic, paprika, basil, oil, salt and pepper in a large skillet. Add in water with the tomato paste dissolved in it.

Bring to a boil over high heat. Simmer mixture, stirring and turning pasta frequently, until pasta is al dente and water has nearly evaporated, about 15 minutes. Serve with olive oil and Parmesan cheese.

Delicious Zucchini Pasta

Serves: 4-5

Prep time: 35 min

Ingredients:

12 oz dry pasta

1 small onion, chopped

2 zucchinis, peeled and cubed

2-3 garlic cloves, crushed

1.5 cups marinara sauce

1 cup black olives, pitted

2 tbsp capers

2 cups water

3 tbsp extra virgin olive oil

1 cup grated Parmezan cheese

1/2 cup fresh dill, finely cut

1 tsp salt

1 tsp fresh black pepper

Directions:

Heat a deep saucepan over medium-high heat. Add in olive oil and gently saute the onion, garlic and zucchinis. Stir in water, marinara sauce and pasta.

Season with salt and black pepper, bring to a boil, cover, and simmer until the pasta is cooked to al dente.

Sprinkle with fresh dill, capers, Parmezan cheese, and serve.

Pasta alla Genovese

Serves: 4-5

Prep time: 30 min

Ingredients:

12 oz small pasta

1-2 medium potatoes, peeled and cut roughly into chunks

4 oz green beans, trimmed

5-6 tbsp pesto

Parmesan cheese, to serve

lemon juice, to serve

Directions:

Prepare the pasta according to package directions.

Cook the potatoes in boiling, salted water until tender, adding the green beans for the last 3-4 minutes of cooking.

Drain the pasta. Drain the beans and potatoes then tip into the pasta together with the pesto and a squeeze of lemon. Toss everything to combine and serve with extra Parmesan.

Pasta with Asparagus

Serves: 4-5

Prep time: 30 min

Ingredients:

12 oz small pasta

1 bunch asparagus trimmed, halved and blanched

3 eggs, whisked

1/2 cup cream

1 tbsp pesto

2 tbsp extra virgin olive oil

Parmesan cheese, to serve

Directions:

Prepare the pasta according to package directions. Drain pasta and return to pan.

Add eggs, olive oil, cream, pesto and parmesan to pasta, tossing quickly over a low heat. Stir in asparagus and serve.

Easy One-Pot Spaghetti

Serves: 4-5

Ingredients:

12 oz spaghetti

1/2 onion, chopped

1 lb boneless chicken breast half, cooked and diced

1 (6 oz) can artichoke hearts, drained

1/2 can chickpeas, drained

2 garlic cloves, crushed

1.5 cups tomato sauce

2 cups water

3 tbsp extra virgin olive oil

1 tsp dried basil

1 tsp dried oregano

1/3 cup fresh parsley, finely cut

1/3 cup crumbled feta cheese

Directions:

Heat a large saucepan over medium-high heat. Add in olive oil and gently saute the onion, garlic, chicken, chickpeas, artichoke hearts, water, and tomato sauce.

Season with salt and black pepper and bring to a boil.

Add in spaghetti, basil and oregano, and stir. Reduce heat and simmer until the spaghetti is cooked to al dente.

Sprinkle with parsley and feta cheese, and serve.

Hearty Lentil Spaghetti

Serves: 4-5

Prep time: 35 min

Ingredients:

12 oz spaghetti

1/2 onion, chopped

1 can brown lentils, rinsed, drained

1 sweet potato, peeled and diced

1-2 garlic cloves, chopped

2 cups tomato sauce

2 cups water

3 tbsp extra virgin olive oil

1/3 cup fresh parsley, finely cut

1 tsp salt

1 cup crumbled feta cheese

Directions:

Heat a deep saucepan over medium-high heat. Add in olive oil and gently saute the onion, garlic, sweet potato and lentils. Add in water and tomato sauce.

Bring to a boil, then add sweet spaghetti and stir. Reduce heat and simmer until the spaghetti is cooked to al dente.

Sprinkle with feta cheese and parsley, adjust seasonings, and serve.

One-Pot Pasta Peperonata

Serves: 4

Prep time 20 min

Ingredients:

12 oz rigatoni, penne or spaghetti

2 red peppers, deseeded and thinly sliced

2 yellow peppers, deseeded and thinly sliced

2 cups onion, finely cut

2 cloves garlic, chopped

1 cup fresh parsley leaves, finely chopped

1 tsp paprika

2 tbsp extra virgin olive oil

salt and freshly ground black pepper

4 1/2 cups water

2 heaped tablespoons mascarpone cheese or crème fraîche, optional

Parmesan cheese, grated, to serve

Directions:

Combine pasta, onion, garlic, peppers, paprika, olive oil, salt and pepper in a large skillet. Add in water. Bring to a boil over high heat.

Boil mixture, stirring and turning pasta frequently, until pasta is al dente and water has nearly evaporated, about 12-15 minutes. Add the mascarpone cheese and stir. Serve with Parmesan.

Mini Shell Bacon and Pea Pasta

Serves: 4

Prep time 20 min

Ingredients:

12 oz mini shell pasta

2-3 slices smoked streaky bacon or pancetta, diced

salt and freshly ground black pepper, to taste

1/2 cup onion, finely cut

2 garlic cloves, chopped

1 cup frozen peas

4 1/2 cups water or chicken broth

2 tbsp extra virgin olive oil

2 heaped tablespoons mascarpone cheese or crème fraîche, optional

2 tbsp fresh dill, finely cut

Parmesan cheese , to serve

Directions:

In a skillet, gently cook bacon for 2-3 minutes, stirring. Add in pasta, onion, garlic, olive oil, salt, pepper, peas and water.

Bring to a boil over high heat. Boil, stirring frequently, until pasta is al dente and water has nearly evaporated, about 15 minutes. Add the mascarpone cheese and dill and stir. Serve with Parmesan.

Pasta with Chicken and Broccoli Pesto

Serves: 4

Prep time 20 min

Ingredients:

12 oz small pasta

1 cup cooked chicken, diced

1 broccoli head, cut in florets

1/2 cup onion, finely cut

2 garlic cloves, chopped

1 red pepper, finely cut

1 tbsp pine nuts

1/2 cup Parmesan cheese

Directions:

Cook the pasta. Boil the broccoli for 2-3 minutes then drain and blend in a food processor.

In a skillet, gently cook the chicken, pepper, garlic and pine nuts for 2-3 minutes, stirring.

Add in the broccoli and warm through, then add the drained pasta and toss. Add the Parmesan cheese and toss to combine.

One-Pot Pasta a La Puttanesca

Serves: 4

Prep time 20 min

Ingredients:

12 oz penne

4 garlic cloves, finely sliced

3 anchovy fillets, chopped

2 fresh red chillies, sliced

½ cup black olives, pitted

2 cups cherry tomatoes, halved

4 1/2 cups water

1 tsp paprika

2 tbsp extra virgin olive oil

salt and freshly ground black pepper, to taste

1/2 cup fresh basil leaves, chopped

Parmesan cheese, to serve

Directions:

Combine pasta, garlic, chillies, basil, paprika, olive oil, olives, anchovies, tomatoes, salt and pepper in a large skillet. Add in water.

Bring to a boil over high heat. Boil mixture, stirring and turning pasta frequently, until pasta is al dente and water has nearly evaporated, about 12-15 minutes. Serve with Parmesan.

Ground Beef Pasta with Garlic-Yogurt Sauce

Serves 5

Prep time: 25 min

Ingredients:

12 oz small pasta

1 lb ground beef

1 onion, finely cut

2 tbsp butter

2 tbsp olive oil

salt and black pepper, to taste

for the sauce:

2 cups yogurt

4-5 garlic cloves, crushed

Directions:

Combine yogurt and garlic.

Gently sauté the onion in olive oil, for 2-3 minutes over medium heat. Add in the ground beef and cook for 10 minutes, or until the meat is cooked through.

Meanwhile, cook pasta according package instructions. Drain and set aside. Melt the butter in a large pot and toss the pasta in it.

Serve pasta, topped with the cooked ground beef and covered with the garlic-yogurt sauce.

Easy Homemade Lasagna

Serves 4-5

Prep time: 40 min.

Ingredients:

1 lb lean ground beef

1 onion, finely chopped

1 carrot, chopped

1 celery rib, chopped

3 garlic cloves, crushed

1 can tomatoes, diced, undrained

1 tbsp tomato paste

1 tbsp dried basil

1/2 cup parsley

1/2 tsp ground black pepper

1/4 tsp salt

1 tsp paprika

1 cup mozzarella cheese, shredded

1 cup Parmesan cheese, shredded

12 no-boil lasagna noodles

Directions:

Heat olive oil in a large pot and gently cook ground beef, onion, carrot, celery, and garlic over medium-high heat until ground meat turns brown.

Bring to a simmer and cook, uncovered, until the liquid is nearly evaporated. Stir in paprika, tomatoes, tomato paste, parsley, black pepper and salt and simmer for 5 minutes.

Combine mozzarella and Parmesan cheese in a medium bowl.

Spread one-third of the meat mixture over the bottom of a greased 13x9x2-inch baking dish. Cover with one-fourth of the cheese mixture. Layer noodles. Repeat layering meat, cheese, and noodles two more times.

Bake in a preheated to 350 F oven for 30 minutes. Sprinkle with remaining cheese mixture and bake, uncovered, about 5 more minutes until the cheese turns gold. Set aside for 10 minutes and serve.

Beef and Spinach Lasagna

Serves 5-6

Prep time: 40 min

Ingredients:

1 lb lean ground beef

1 bag frozen spinach

1 onion, chopped

1 can tomatoes

2-3 garlic cloves, crushed

1 tsp dried basil

1 tsp dried oregano

1 cup ricotta cheese

2 cup mozzarella cheese, shredded

12 no-cook lasagna noodles

Directions:

In a skillet, sauté onion and garlic for a few minutes. Add in beef and cook over medium heat until the meat is no longer pink. Stir in tomatoes, basil and oregano. Simmer for 10-12 minutes.

In a bowl, combine the thawed spinach with half the ricotta and mozzarella cheese.

Spread one-third of the meat mixture over the bottom of a greased 13x9x2-inch baking dish. Sprinkle with one-fourth of the spinach-cheese mixture. Top with noodles. Repeat layering meat, spinach mixture, and noodles two more times.

Bake for 40 minutes in a preheated to 350 F oven. Sprinkle with the remaining cheese mixture. Bake, uncovered, about 5 minutes until the cheese turns golden. Set aside for at least 10 minutes before serving.

Baked Ground Beef Pasta

Serves 6

Prep time: 25 min

Ingredients:

12 oz small pasta

1 lb ground beef

2 onions, finely chopped

4 garlic cloves, chopped

3-4 mushrooms, chopped

5-6 gherkins, chopped

1 small tomato, diced

1/2 cup parsley leaves, chopped

1 can mushroom soup

salt and black pepper, to taste

1 cup mozzarella cheese, grated

1 egg, whisked

Directions:

Prepare the pasta according to package directions. Drain and place in an ovenproof baking dish.

Heat olive oil in a large pot and gently sauté the onion until transparent. Add in ground beef, mushrooms, garlic and tomato. Stir and cook on low heat for about 10 minutes. When the meat is almost done, add in the gherkins and parsley.

Toss everything with the pasta. Add in the mushroom soup and stir to combine.

Whisk the egg with mozzarella cheese and spread all over the pasta equally. Bake in a preheated to 350 F oven for 10 minutes or until the cheese turns golden.

Baked Pasta with Broccoli, Olives and Pancetta

Serves 6

Prep time: 25 min

Ingredients:

12 oz small pasta

1 1/2 pounds broccoli, cut into small florets

1 lb cherry tomatoes

one 4 oz slice of pancetta, finely diced

1 cup black olives, pitted and halved

1 onion, finely cut

2 garlic cloves, chopped

9-10 fresh basil leaves, chopped

2 cups fresh ricotta cheese

3/4 cup grated Parmesan cheese

2 tbsp extra virgin olive oil

salt and black pepper, to taste

Directions:

Preheat the oven to 425 F and oil an ovenproof baking dish. Add in the tomatoes, broccoli, garlic and basil. Sprinkle with half the olive oil and season with salt and pepper. Roast for about 20 minutes, until softened.

Prepare the pasta according to package directions and toss with the roasted tomatoes, broccoli and garlic.

Meanwhile, in a large, deep skillet, heat the remaining 1 tablespoon of olive oil. Add in the pancetta and cook over moderately high heat, stirring occasionally, until browned and nearly crisp, about 5 minutes. Stir and add the onion. Cook on low heat, stirring occasionally, until softened, about 5 minutes.

Toss everything in the baking dish. Add in the ricotta and Parmesan cheese and stir to combine.

Bake in a preheated to 350 F oven for 10 minutes or until the cheese turns golden.

Baked Penne with with Spinach, Feta and Fontina

Serves 6

Prep time: 25 min

Ingredients:

1 lb penne

1 10 oz package frozen spinach, thawed

1 cup cherry tomatoes, halved

2 garlic cloves, chopped

9-10 fresh basil leaves, chopped

2 cups crumbled feta cheese

6 oz fontina, grated

3/4 cup grated Parmesan cheese

2 tbsp extra virgin olive oil

1/2 tsp nutmeg

salt and black pepper, to taste

Directions:

Preheat the oven to 350 F and oil a ceramic or glass baking dish.

Prepare the pasta according to package directions and put it in the prepared baking dish. Toss with 1 tablespoon of the oil.

Meanwhile, put the spinach in a food processor and puree with the garlic, feta, half Parmesan cheese, the nutmeg, salt, and pepper. Stir in half the fontina.

Toss everything in the baking dish. Add the cherry tomatoes and stir. Top with the remaining fontina and Parmesan. Bake the pasta until the cheese turns golden, 15-20 minutes.

Easy Three-Cheese Pasta with Chicken and Mushrooms

Serves 6

Prep time: 25 min

Ingredients:

1 lb small pasta

9-10 white button mushrooms, chopped

2 cups cooked chicken, diced

1/2 onion, finely cut

2 garlic cloves, chopped

9-10 fresh basil leaves, chopped

2 cups Ricotta cheese

6 oz fontina, grated

3/4 cup grated Parmesan cheese

3 tbsp extra virgin olive oil

1/2 tsp dried oregano

salt and black pepper, to taste

Directions:

Preheat the oven to 350 F and oil an ovenproof baking dish.

Prepare the pasta according to package directions and put it in the prepared baking dish. Toss with 2 tablespoons of the oil.

Meanwhile, in a large, deep skillet, heat the remaining 1 tablespoon of olive oil. Add in the onion and mushrooms and cook over moderately high heat, stirring occasionally, until softened, about 5 minutes. Add the garlic and chicken. Cook on low heat, stirring occasionally, about 2 minutes. Add the Ricotta cheese and half the Parmesan and fontina. Stir to combine.

Toss everything in the baking dish. Top with the remaining fontina and Parmesan. Bake the pasta until the cheese turns golden, 15-20 minutes.

Greek-style Baked Pasta

Serves 5

Prep time: 25 min

Ingredients:

12 oz small pasta

1 lb lean ground lamb

3 cups marinara sauce

1 onion, finely cut

2 garlic cloves, chopped

2 tbsp olive oil

2 eggs

1 tsp nutmeg

3 cups fresh ricotta cheese

3/4 cup grated Parmesan cheese

salt and black pepper, to taste

Directions:

Gently sauté the onion in olive oil, for 2-3 minutes over medium heat. Add in the ground lamb and garlic and cook for 10 minutes, or until the meat is cooked through. Stir in the marinara sauce. Season with salt and pepper, to taste.

In a blender, blend 2 cups of the ricotta with the eggs, nutmeg and 1/2 cup of the Parmesan cheese until smooth

Meanwhile, cook the pasta according package instructions. Drain and set aside in an oiled baking dish.

Add the lamb mixture to the pasta and toss to combine. Pour the ricotta mixture on top and sprinkle with the remaining Parmesan cheese. Bake the pasta until the cheese turns golden, 15-20 minutes.

Ricotta and Spinach Cannelloni

Serves 5

Prep time: 25 min

Ingredients:

1 lb dried cannelloni tubes

1 lb chopped spinach

1 onion, finely cut

1 garlic clove, chopped

1/2 cup green olives, chopped

1 lb mascarpone

1 lb ricotta

1 cup milk

1/4 cup toasted pine nuts

1 tsp nutmeg

1 tsp smoked paprika

3 cups fresh ricotta cheese

1/2 cup grated Parmesan cheese

2 tbsp extra virgin olive oil

salt and black pepper, to taste

Directions:

Gently sauté the onion and garlic in olive oil, for 2-3 minutes over medium heat. Add in the spinach and cook for 3-4 minutes, or until it wilts. Season with salt and pepper to taste and add the paprika, pine nuts and green olives.

Set aside to cool and stir in the ricotta cheese.

In a bowl, whisk the mascarpone with the milk, nutmeg, the Parmesan and some salt. Spread half of this mixture into a large ovenproof dish.

Spoon some of the kale filling in each cannelloni tube using a teaspoon, and place the tubes in the dish, snugly together, on top of the mascarpone mixture.

Pour the other half of the mascarpone mixture over the cannelloni tubes, and sprinkle with Parmesan.

Bake in a preheated to 350 F oven for 30 minutes, or until the top is crisp, the sauce is bubbling and the pasta soft.

FREE BONUS RECIPES: 20 Superfood Paleo and Vegan Smoothies for Vibrant Health and Easy Weight Loss

Kale and Kiwi Smoothie

Serves: 2

Prep time: 2-3 min

Ingredients:

2-3 ice cubes

1 cup orange juice

1 small pear, peeled and chopped

2 kiwi, peeled and chopped

2-3 kale leaves

2-3 dates, pitted

Directions:

Combine all ingredients in a high speed blender and blend until smooth.

Delicious Broccoli Smoothie

Serves: 2

Prep time: 2-3 min

Ingredients:

2-3 frozen broccoli florets

1 cup coconut milk

1 banana, peeled and chopped

1 cup pineapple, cut

1 peach, chopped

1 tsp cinnamon

Directions:

Combine all ingredients in a high speed blender and blend until smooth.

Papaya Smoothie

Serves: 2

Prep time: 2-3 min

Ingredients:

2-3 frozen broccoli florets

1 cup orange juice

1 small ripe avocado, peeled, cored and diced

1 cup papaya

1 cup fresh strawberries

Directions:

Combine all ingredients in a high speed blender and blend until smooth.

Beet and Papaya Smoothie

Serves: 2

Prep time: 2-3 min

Ingredients:

3-4 ice cubes

1 cup orange juice

1 banana, peeled and chopped

1 cup papaya

1 small beet, peeled and cut

Directions:

Combine all ingredients in a high speed blender and blend until smooth.

Lean Green Smoothie

Serves: 2

Prep time: 2-3 min

Ingredients:

1 frozen banana, chopped

1 cup orange juice

2-3 kale leaves, stems removed

1 small cucumber, peeled and chopped

1/2 cup fresh parsley leaves

½ tsp grated ginger

Directions:

Combine all ingredients in a high speed blender and blend until smooth.

Easy Antioxidant Smoothie

Serves: 2

Prep time: 2-3 min

Ingredients:

2-3 frozen broccoli florets

1 cup orange juice

2 plums, cut

1 cup raspberries

1 tsp ginger powder

Directions:

Combine all ingredients in a high speed blender and blend until smooth.

Healthy Purple Smoothie

Serves: 2

Prep time: 2-3 min

Ingredients:

2-3 frozen broccoli florets

1 cup water

1/2 avocado, peeled and chopped

3 plums, chopped

1 cup blueberries

Directions:

Combine all ingredients in a high speed blender and blend until smooth.

Mom's Favorite Kale Smoothie

Serves: 2

Prep time: 2-3 min

Ingredients:

2-3 ice cubes

1½ cup orange juice

1 green small apple, cut

½ cucumber, chopped

2-3 leaves kale

½ cup raspberries

Directions:

Combine all ingredients in a high speed blender and blend until smooth.

Creamy Green Smoothie

Serves: 2

Prep time: 2-3 min

Ingredients:

1 frozen banana

1 cup coconut milk

1 small pear, chopped

1 cup baby spinach

1 cup grapes

1 tbsp coconut butter

1 tsp vanilla extract

Directions:

Combine all ingredients in a high speed blender and blend until smooth.

Strawberry and Arugula Smoothie

Serves: 2

Prep time: 2-3 min

Ingredients:

2 cups frozen strawberries

1 cup unsweetened almond milk

10-12 arugula leaves

1/2 tsp ground cinnamon

Directions:

Combine ice, almond milk, strawberries, arugula and cinnamon in a high speed blender. Blend until smooth and serve.

Emma's Amazing Smoothie

Serves: 2

Prep time: 2-3 min

Ingredients:

1 frozen banana, chopped

1 cup orange juice

1 large nectarine, sliced

1/2 zucchini, peeled and chopped

2-3 dates, pitted

Directions:

Combine all ingredients in a high speed blender and blend until smooth.

Good-To-Go Morning Smoothie

Serves: 2

Prep time: 2-3 min

Ingredients:

1 cup frozen strawberries

1 cup apple juice

1 banana, chopped

1 cup raw asparagus, chopped

1 tbsp ground flaxseed

Directions:

Combine all ingredients in a high speed blender and blend until smooth.

Endless Energy Smoothie

Serves: 2

Prep time: 2-3 min

Ingredients:

1 frozen banana, chopped

1 1/2 cup green tea

1 cup chopped pineapple

2 raw asparagus spears, chopped

1 lime, juiced

1 tbsp chia seeds

Directions:

Combine all ingredients in a high speed blender and blend until smooth.

High-fibre Fruit Smoothie

Serves: 2

Prep time: 2-3 min

Ingredients:

1 frozen banana, chopped

1 cup orange juice

2 cups chopped papaya

1 cup shredded cabbage

1 tbsp chia seeds

Directions:

Combine all ingredients in a high speed blender and blend until smooth.

Nutritious Green Smoothie

Serves: 2

Prep time: 2-3 min

Ingredients:

2-3 frozen broccoli florets

1 cup apple juice

1 large pear, chopped

1 kiwi, peeled and chopped

1 cup spinach leaves

1-2 dates, pitted

Directions:

Combine all ingredients in a high speed blender and blend until smooth.

Apricot, Strawberry and Banana Smoothie

Serves: 2

Prep time: 2-3 min

Ingredients:

1 frozen banana

1 1/2 cup almond milk

5 dried apricots

1 cup fresh strawberries

Directions:

Combine all ingredients in a high speed blender and blend until smooth.

Spinach and Green Apple Smoothie

Serves: 2

Prep time: 2-3 min

Ingredients:

3-4 ice cubes

1 cup unsweetened almond milk

1 banana, peeled and chopped

2 green apples, peeled and chopped

1 cup raw spinach leaves

3-4 dates, pitted

1 tsp grated ginger

Directions:

Combine all ingredients in a high speed blender and blend until smooth.

Superfood Blueberry Smoothie

Serves: 2

Prep time: 2-3 min

Ingredients:

2-3 cubes frozen spinach

1 cup green tea

1 banana

2 cups blueberries

1 tbsp ground flaxseed

Directions:

Combine all ingredients in a high speed blender and blend until smooth.

Zucchini and Blueberry Smoothie

Serves: 2

Prep time: 2-3 min

Ingredients:

1 cup frozen blueberries

1 cup unsweetened almond milk

1 banana

1 zucchini, peeled and chopped

Directions:

Combine all ingredients in a high speed blender and blend until smooth.

Tropical Spinach Smoothie

Serves: 2

Prep time: 2-3 min

Ingredients:

1/2 cup crushed ice or 3-4 ice cubes

1 cup coconut milk

1 mango, peeled and diced

1 cup fresh spinach leaves

4-5 dates, pitted

1/2 tsp vanilla extract

Directions:

Combine all ingredients in a high speed blender and blend until smooth.

About the Author

Alissa Grey is a fitness and nutrition enthusiast who loves to teach people about losing weight and feeling better about themselves. She lives in a small French village in the foothills of a beautiful mountain range with her husband, three teenage kids, two free spirited dogs, and various other animals.

Alissa Grey is incredibly lucky to be able to cook and eat natural foods, mostly grown nearby, something she's done since she was a teenager. She enjoys yoga, running, reading, hanging out with her family, and growing organic vegetables and herbs.

Printed in Great Britain
by Amazon